The Young Scientist Investigates

The Human Body

by
Terry Jennings

CHILDRENS PRESS®
CHICAGO

Library of Congress Cataloging-in-Publication Data

Jennings, Terry J.
    The human body / by Terry Jennings.
      p.   cm. — (The Young scientist investigates.)
    Includes index.
    ISBN 0-516-08404-6
    1. Body, Human—Juvenile literature. 2. Anatomy, Human—
Juvenile literature. I. Title. II. Series: Jennings, Terry J. Young
scientist investigates.
    QM27.J46   1988
    611—dc 19   88-22859
                                              CIP
                                              AC

North American edition published in 1989 by Regensteiner
Publishing Enterprises, Inc.

© Terry Jennings 1986
First published 1986 by Oxford University Press

Printed in the United States of America
1 2 3 4 5 6 7 8 9 10 R 98 97 96 95 94 93 92 91 90 89

The Human Body

Contents

What we are made of

Did you learn this nursery rhyme when you were small?

> What are little boys made of?
> What are little boys made of?
> Frogs and snails, and puppy dogs' tails
> That's what little boys are made of.
> What are little girls made of?
> What are little girls made of?
> Sugar and spice and everything nice.
> That's what little girls are made of!

Thank goodness, for the sake of boys, this nursery rhyme is wrong! Girls and boys are made of the same things. They are made up of cells. Cells are the building blocks of our body. Your cells are so tiny that they can be seen only with a microscope. But you have millions and millions of them.

There are many different kinds of cells. Your bones are made of one kind of cell, your muscles of another. There are several kinds of cells in your blood and skin. Your brain and nerves are made of nerve cells. Different cells have different jobs to do. But they all work together to help make us what we are.

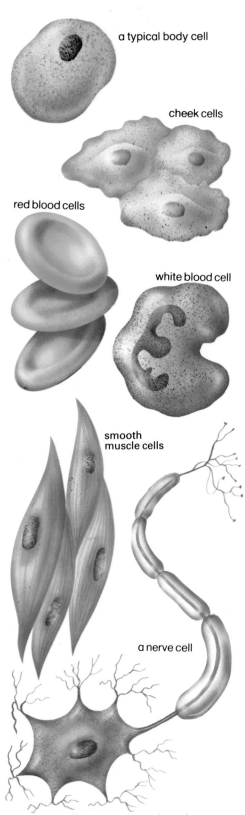

a typical body cell

cheek cells

red blood cells

white blood cell

smooth muscle cells

a nerve cell

Cells seen through a microscope

The skin

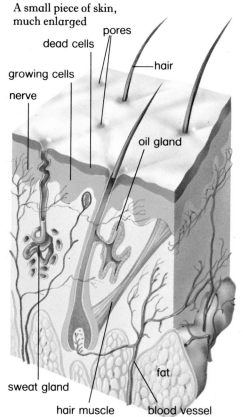

A small piece of skin, much enlarged

- dead cells
- pores
- hair
- growing cells
- nerve
- oil gland
- sweat gland
- hair muscle
- fat
- blood vessel

Freckles

Although your skin is your body's covering, it does much more than stop your insides from falling out. Skin is waterproof and it keeps germs out of your body. It helps keep the body at the right temperature. When we are hot, more blood passes to the skin, to carry the heat away. And sweat, produced by sweat glands in the skin, helps keep us cool. The sweat flows out of openings or pores on the surface of the skin. When it is cold, less blood flows to the skin and less heat is lost.

Your skin is made of many layers of cells. The outer layers are dead or dying cells. Many of these come off when you wash or rub your skin. But new cells are growing underneath all the time. Every hair on your body grows from a tiny root under your skin. Near the hair roots are glands that make an oily substance to keep the skin waterproof.

Certain cells in your skin contain a dark substance called melanin. How much melanin you have usually depends on how much your parents have. Sunshine helps to make melanin too. When you go out in the sun, you may get darker because melanin is formed in the skin. In some people melanin makes little patches, or freckles. People who always have a lot of melanin in their skin are brown or black in color. People with less melanin have lighter skin. But whether we have dark skin or light skin, with or without freckles, we are all alike inside.

Bones and skeletons

Inside our body we have a skeleton made from bone. Some animals have a skeleton on the outside of their body. The crab's shell is really a skeleton. As a crab grows it has to shed its shell and grow a bigger one. Our skeletons grow larger as we grow. We never get too large for our skeleton.

The skeleton is very important in many ways. It holds the body upright and gives it its shape and strength. Without a skeleton our body would be as floppy and limp as that of an earthworm or jellyfish. The skeleton also protects the delicate parts of the body. The skull protects the brain. The ribs and breastbone protect the heart and lungs. Safely inside the backbone is the delicate spinal cord.

A skeleton is made up of long bones, short bones, and some bones that have strange shapes. Altogether there are 206 bones in your skeleton. Not all bones are solid. The long bones of our arms and legs are hollow. They are filled with marrow. Marrow is a substance that helps make blood. If our bones were not hollow, they would be too heavy for us to move. A hollow bone is strong but light.

Bone is a living, growing substance. That is why a broken bone can mend again.

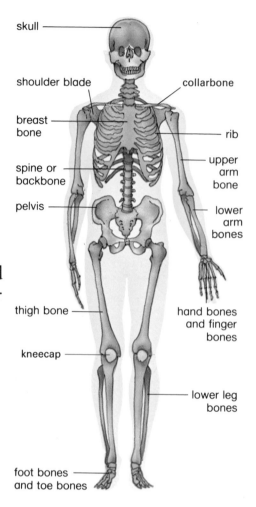

Human skeleton

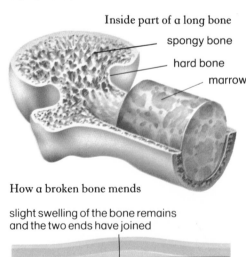

Inside part of a long bone

spongy bone

hard bone

marrow

How a broken bone mends

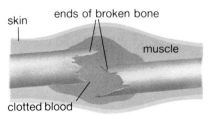

skin

ends of broken bone

muscle

clotted blood

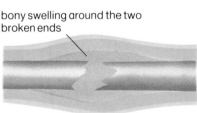

bony swelling around the two broken ends

slight swelling of the bone remains and the two ends have joined

Muscles and movement

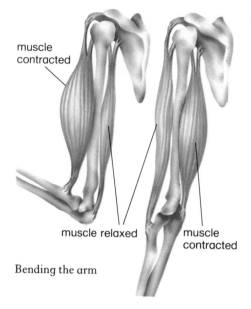

muscle contracted

muscle relaxed

muscle contracted

Bending the arm

Bones will not bend. We can move our arms, legs, hands, fingers, toes, and other parts of our body only because the bones have joints between them. The power to move our bones comes from our muscles. Muscles pull on the bones to move them.

Muscles cannot push, they can only pull. When a muscle pulls it becomes shorter and fatter. The muscle is said to contract. To pull the bone back there has to be another muscle. You can feel the muscle pulling your forearm if you hold your arm like this (below right). You can feel the muscle becoming shorter and fatter. Your arm is pulled straight again when the muscle at the back of the arm contracts and the muscle at the front of the arm relaxes. Muscles always work in pairs.

Sometimes the bones that are to be moved are a long way from the muscles. Then the muscle pulls on a string-like tendon. The other end of the tendon pulls on the bone. A tendon works like the chain on a bicycle's brakes.

Tendons in the hand

If you look at a piece of meat, you can see muscle. Muscle is the lean part of the meat. Muscles get their energy from the food and oxygen carried to them by the blood. That is why lean meat or muscle is red in color.

Teeth

When a baby is born, it already has teeth hidden beneath its gums. Between the ages of 6 months and 3 years, the baby's teeth appear. Eventually a baby has 20 teeth. These are called baby teeth.

A baby's first teeth

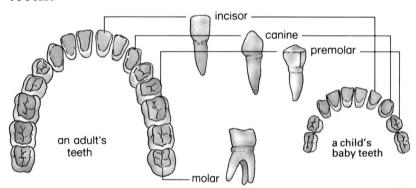

incisor
canine
premolar
an adult's teeth
a child's baby teeth
molar

Grown-ups have 32 teeth. These are often called the permanent teeth. They have to last the rest of your life. Between the ages of about 6 and 12 years, the baby teeth start to loosen. As they fall out the permanent teeth come through in their place.

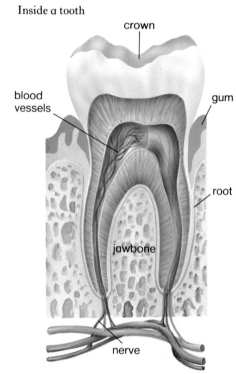

Inside a tooth

crown
blood vessels
gum
root
jawbone
nerve

Our teeth are designed for the work they do. The front teeth are called incisors. They bite and cut the food. The pointed side teeth are known as canines. They tear and shred the food. The back teeth are called premolars and molars. They chew and grind the food so that it becomes a pulpy mass that can be easily swallowed.

A tooth has two main parts. The crown is the white part of the tooth you can see. Under the crown is the root. This is hidden in the gums. Inside a tooth there are tiny blood vessels and a nerve. A tooth aches when something affects this nerve.

Digestion

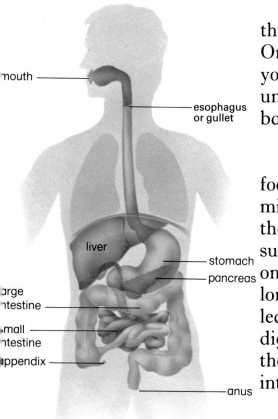

We need food to keep us healthy and to enable us to grow. Food keeps us warm and gives us the energy to do all the things we do. But food cannot be used by the body as it is. It has to be broken down so that it can be carried in the blood. The breaking down of food into bits small enough to pass into the blood is called digestion.

Above, some foods that give us energy and *right*, some foods that help us to grow

Digestion happens in a long tube that runs through your body. This tube has two openings. One is the mouth. Here food and drinks enter your body. The other opening is the anus. There unused food leaves the body when you go to the bathroom.

Digestion begins in the mouth. As we chew food with our teeth, a liquid called saliva is mixed with the food. This has a chemical in it that turns some of the starch in the food to sugar. In the stomach another chemical carries on digesting the food. After this the food enters a long coiled tube called the intestine. Here at least 17 more chemicals finish the work of digesting the food. These chemicals come from the liver, the pancreas, and from the wall of the intestine itself.

mouth

esophagus or gullet

liver

stomach

pancreas

arge ntestine

mall ntestine

ppendix

anus

Digestive system of a child

The digested food passes through the walls of the intestine. It goes into the blood. The blood takes the digested food to all parts of the body.

Air to breathe

We need air to stay alive. When you breathe, air goes into your nose or mouth. The air passes down your windpipe to the lungs. We have two lungs, one on each side of our heart.

The lungs cannot take in air by themselves. They do not have muscles. Air goes into our lungs because our chest gets bigger. This is partly because muscles move our ribs. And also because a sheet of muscle under the ribs, called the diaphragm, flattens. When the chest becomes bigger, air rushes down the windpipe and fills the lungs. When you exhale, the chest relaxes and gets smaller again. Air is then forced out of the lungs and out of the body.

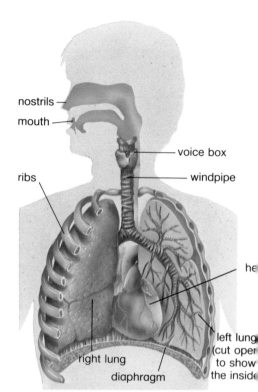

nostrils
mouth
voice box
ribs
windpipe
he[
left lung (cut open to show the inside)
right lung
diaphragm

The chest and lungs

How we inhale and exhale

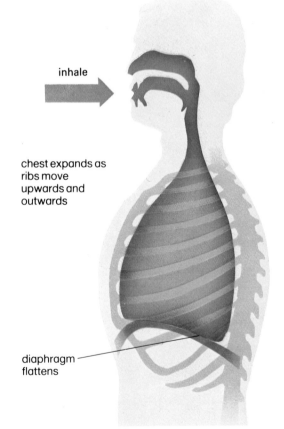

inhale

chest expands as ribs move upwards and outwards

diaphragm flattens

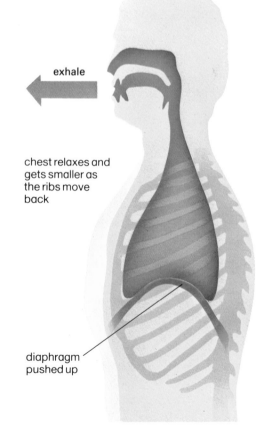

exhale

chest relaxes and gets smaller as the ribs move back

diaphragm pushed up

8

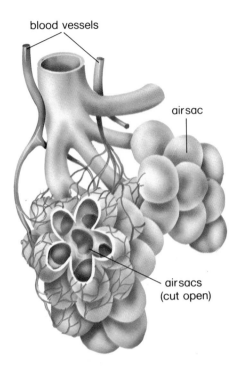

blood vessels

airsac

airsacs
(cut open)

Part of the interior of the lung

The most important gas in the air is oxygen. The tubes inside each lung are arranged rather like the branches and twigs of a tree. There are tiny little swellings called airsacs at the end of each of the smallest tubes. Inside these little airsacs some of the oxygen in the air passes into very small blood vessels. The blood carries the oxygen to all parts of our body. Oxygen combines with food in the cells of our body. Oxygen and food make the energy we need.

Two of the waste substances from when the food gives up its energy are water, and a gas called carbon dioxide. These are carried to our lungs by the blood. They go into the air when we breathe out.

The heart and the blood circulation

The blood is driven round the body by the heart. The heart is a very powerful pump. It is made of muscle. The heart beats about 70 times a minute in adults. It beats faster than this in children. With each beat the heart pumps about a cupful of blood around the body.

When the blood leaves the heart, it travels in tubes called arteries. These take the blood all over the body. The blood moving along arteries does so in jerks as it is pumped by the heart. Where an artery comes near the skin you can feel the blood moving in jerks. We call these jerks the pulse. The blood in arteries is bright red because it contains oxygen. Arteries divide up eventually into tiny tubes called capillaries. Capillaries carry the blood to every nook and corner of the body. If a scratch bleeds it is because you have torn some of the capillaries.

After the blood has given up its oxygen and food to the cells of the body, the blood travels back to the heart. The blood travels back to the heart first in capillaries and then in larger tubes called veins. The blood in veins is a dark color because it has given up its oxygen.

The way the blood travels round and round the body is called the blood circulation. The blood circulation is controlled by the heart. The heart is a very special pump. No other pump can work for 70 or 80 years or more without stopping or resting.

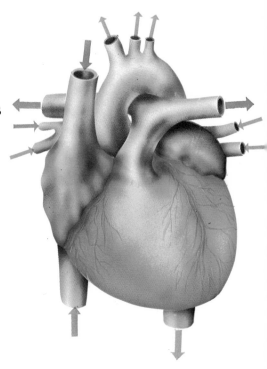

The heart

How the blood circulates, much simplified

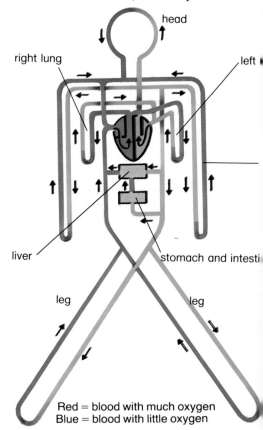

head

right lung

left

liver

stomach and intesti

leg   leg

Red = blood with much oxygen
Blue = blood with little oxygen

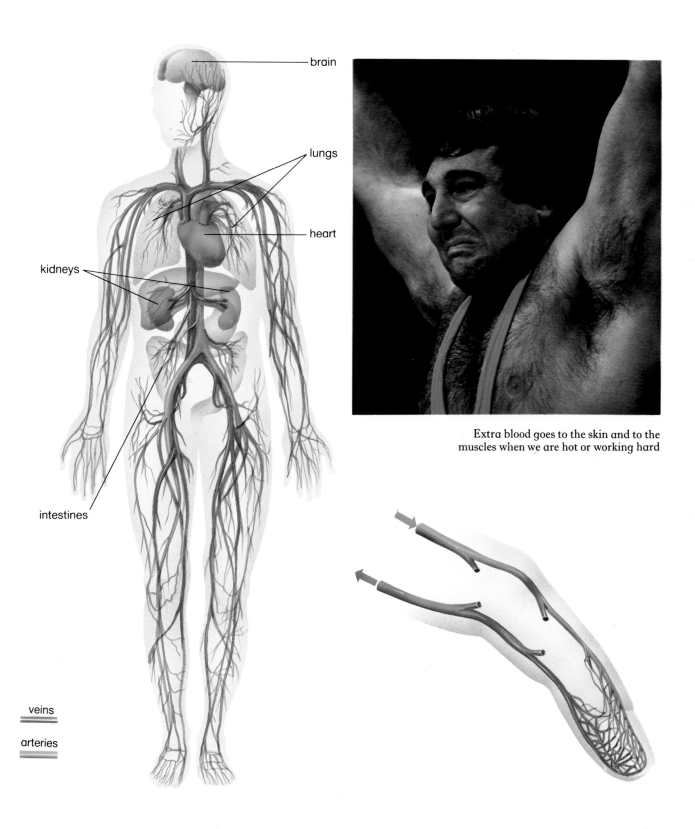

brain

lungs

heart

kidneys

intestines

veins

arteries

Extra blood goes to the skin and to the muscles when we are hot or working hard

The main blood vessels of the body

Some of the blood vessels to the finger

Blood

Blood is not just a liquid. Floating in blood are millions and millions of tiny cells, too small to be seen without a microscope. Most of the cells are red. It is these which make the blood look red. Mixed in with the red blood cells are smaller numbers of white cells.

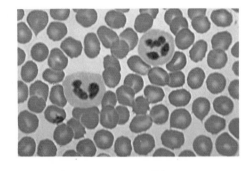

Blood has many jobs to do. The liquid part of the blood carries heat and digested food to all parts of the body. It carries waste materials to the kidneys. It carries carbon dioxide from the rest of the body to the lungs. Also carried in the blood are chemical messengers called hormones. These help the brain control the different parts of the body.

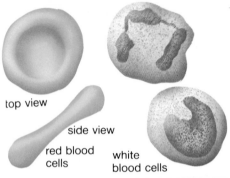

top view

side view

red blood cells

white blood cells

germ

1   white blood cell
2–4 cell engulfs germ
5   germ now digested

The red blood cells carry oxygen from the lungs all round the body. White blood cells have the task of killing germs that enter the body. When a cut has germs in it, large numbers of white blood cells move toward the cut. The white cells surround and kill the germs. In doing this many of the white cells die. Their dead bodies form part of the matter or pus which comes out of an infected scratch or wound. Some white blood cells make chemicals which destroy the poisons made by germs that make us ill.

When you cut yourself, substances in the blood help it to clot when the blood meets the air. A scab is formed. This protects the cut until new skin can grow over it.

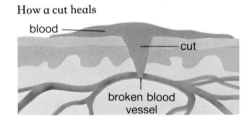

How a cut heals

blood

cut

broken blood vessel

scab forms

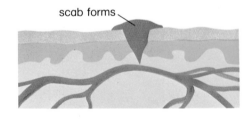

scar remains, blood vessel is healed

Do you remember?

(Look for the answers in the part of the book you have just been reading if you do not know them.)

1 What are we all made of?

2 What does the skin produce to help to cool us?

3 What is the name of the dark substance in skin cells?

4 Name three delicate parts of the body that are protected by the skeleton.

5 Why are some long bones hollow?

6 How do muscles move bones?

7 What do we call it when a muscle becomes shorter and fatter?

8 What is a tendon?

9 What do we call the first teeth we have?

10 What do the incisor teeth do?

11 Which teeth tear and shred food?

12 What are the two main parts of a tooth?

13 Why do we need food?

14 Why does food have to be digested?

15 What happens to our chest when we inhale?

16 What is the heart made of?

17 When blood leaves the heart, what does it travel in?

18 What is the blood circulation?

19 What do red blood cells carry?

20 How do white blood cells protect us from germs?

Things to do

1 **Studying cells.** It is not easy to see human cells, even if you have a microscope. However, plants, like animals, also are made of cells. You can see the cells of an onion quite easily with a microscope.

Cut a slice of onion. Carefully peel off a tiny piece of the thin skin. Lay this skin on a microscope slide. Place a drop of water on the center of the skin. Gently put a coverslip over it.

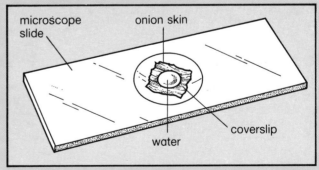

What does the onion skin look like under the microscope? Can you see the tiny boxlike cells? Some human cells look a little like this, although plant cells have tough walls around them while animal cells are surrounded only by a thin membrane.

2   How much skin do you have? This is a difficult thing to measure accurately.

One way is to lie down on a large sheet of paper squared into inches. Keep very still while a friend carefully draws around your body.

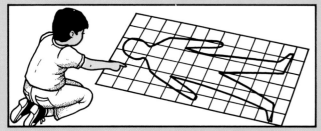

Add up all the squares inside the line. If more than half a square is inside the line, count it in the total. If less than half a square is inside the line do not count it.

What is the total number of squares inside the line? If you double the number you will know how much skin you have.

Is your answer correct? Why? Can you think of any other ways of finding out how much skin you have?

3   Examine your skin. Use a hand lens or magnifying glass to examine the skin of your hand. Can you see the pores?

Where on your body do you have (a) very thin skin; (b) thick skin? Why do you think lips and gums are red in color?

4   Make a study of fingerprints. Make a study of fingerprints the way detectives do. You can make fingerprints using the kind of ink pad that is used for rubber stamps.

Choose one that has washable ink on it. You could also try black shoe polish. Wash the shoe polish off afterwards with a little soap.

Roll your finger gently on the pad or in the polish. Then roll your finger on a piece of white drawing paper. You might have to practice several times to get clear fingerprints that are not smudged.

Are the fingerprints of any two of your fingers the same? Are your fingerprints the same as anyone else's in your class?

The four main kinds of fingerprints are shown in the pictures. Which type are your fingerprints?

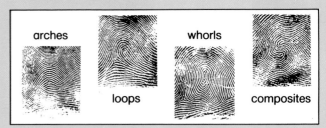

5   Your skeleton. Look at the picture of a human skeleton on page 4. Try to find these bones by feeling them on your own body:

skull	backbone
ribs	thigh bone
shoulder blade	lower leg bones
collarbone	upper arm bones
kneecap	lower arm bones
hips	

How are your arm bones like your leg bones?

Use a tape measure or ruler and string to measure some of your bones on your own skeleton.

Which is longer, the upper arm bone or the lower arm bones? Which is longer, the thigh bone or the lower leg bones?

Measure these bones to find out. Is the answer you find true for everyone?

6   Cut a bone in half. Collect a large fresh bone from the butcher. Ask the butcher to cut the bone in half with a hacksaw. Look at the hollow part in the middle of the bone. Can you see the marrow? What is it like?

Would you expect to find marrow in a bird's bones? Why?

7   Tendons. Look carefully at the back of your hand while you wiggle your fingers. Can you see the tendons moving? Can you find the muscles they are joined to?

There is another thick tendon behind your knee. Can you find that?

8   Make a model of the arm. Make a model showing how the bones and muscles of the arm work.

Cut three pieces of sturdy cardboard. Two pieces should be about 10 inches long and 1 inch wide. The other piece can be a little shorter.

Use brass paper fasteners to fix the three pieces of cardboard together. Use two fasteners to join the shoulder blade to the upper arm. Use one fastener to join the upper and lower arm bones at the elbow.

Use a knitting needle or nail to make four small holes at A, B, C, and D. Tie two

lengths of thin string to A and B, and thread the other ends of the string through C and D. The strings are to represent muscles.

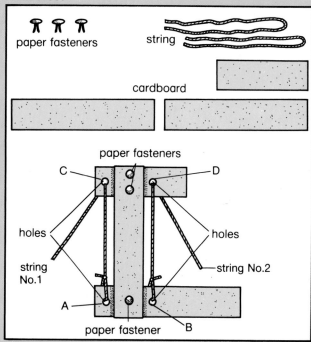

Start with the model's lower arm bone in the position shown in our picture. Pull on the end of string number 1. What happens to the lower arm bone? Now pull on string number 2. What happens to the lower arm bone?

Make a similar model showing how the head moves on the neck.

9   How much does your chest move when you inhale and exhale? If you are wearing a jacket or sweater, take it off. Ask a friend to measure your chest by running a tape measure around your chest under your armpits. What is the measurement?

Now take a deep breath and hold it while your friend again measures your chest. What is the measurement? Now exhale.

What does your chest measure now?

What is the difference in the size of your chest when you inhale and exhale?

10   The air we exhale. Breathe onto a mirror. The mist that collects on the surface of the mirror is water vapor that has come from your lungs.

Now read what temperature a wall thermometer says. Place your mouth about an inch away from the thermometer. Exhale hard. What temperature does the thermometer say now? Why is there a difference?

11   How many teeth do you have?
Study your own teeth in a mirror. Make a record chart of your teeth like the one below. Each little square is for one tooth. Grown-ups can have 32 teeth (16 in each jaw). How many do you have?

Fill in your tooth chart like this:

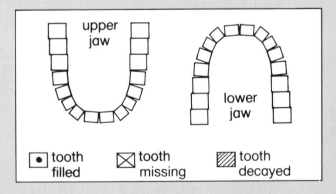

If a tooth is filled put a small black circle.
If a tooth is missing put a cross.
If a tooth is decayed shade it in.

How does your tooth chart compare with those of your friends? Who has the most healthy teeth?

12   A model stethoscope. The doctor uses a stethoscope to listen to the sounds your heart and lungs make. If you have two plastic funnels and a piece of rubber or plastic tubing, you can make a simple stethoscope. Join the funnels to the tube like this.

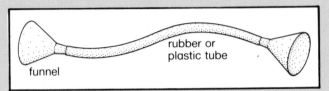

rubber or plastic tube

funnel

Put one funnel on a friend's chest. Put the other funnel up to your ear. Can you hear the beat of your friend's heart? The sounds travel along the tube to your ear. What does a beating heart sound like?

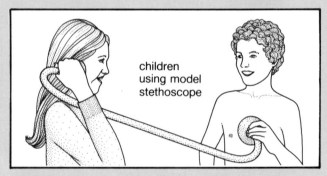

children using model stethoscope

13   A pulse counter. It is often easier to count your pulse if you make this simple counter. Carefully push a matchstick onto the point of a tack. Rest the tack on your left wrist behind your thumb. Watch the matchstick sway backward and forward each time your pulse beats.

Can you find a pulse anywhere else on your body other than on your wrist?

Getting rid of waste

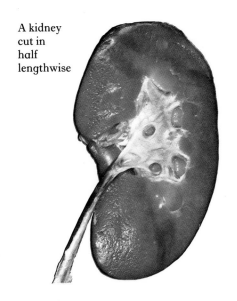

A kidney cut in half lengthwise

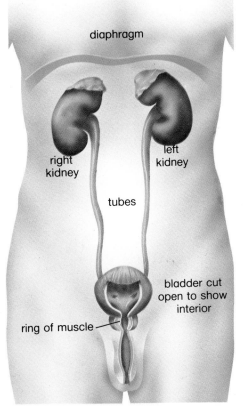

The kidneys and the bladder

diaphragm

right kidney

left kidney

tubes

bladder cut open to show interior

ring of muscle

Our body produces a lot of waste chemicals. We have already seen how waste carbon dioxide is removed by our lungs. Sweat glands in the skin also remove some waste chemicals. But most waste chemicals are removed by the kidneys.

We have two kidneys. Each is about 4 inches long. They lie in the small of the back just in front of the backbone. Each kidney is made up of thousands of coiling tubes. Every time the heart beats, some of the blood passes through these tubes in the kidneys. There the tubes filter off waste chemicals from the blood. These chemicals would poison us if they were not removed. The blood leaves the kidneys clean and pure. Meanwhile, the waste chemicals, dissolved in water, drip down a long tube running from each kidney to a bag called the bladder. These watery wastes are the yellow liquid we call urine.

The urine is stored in the bladder. A ring of muscle closes the bottom of the bladder. It stops the urine from leaking out all the time. When you go to the bathroom, the muscle relaxes so that the urine can flow out. In girls, the urine leaves the body through an opening between the legs. In the case of boys, the urine leaves the body through a fleshy tube called the penis.

Speaking and hearing

We are able to speak because in our throat we have a voice box. This is the lump some people call the Adam's Apple . Inside the voice box are folds of muscle called vocal cords. When we want to speak or sing we make our vocal cords vibrate. We do this by forcing air from our lungs over the vocal cords. When the vocal cords vibrate they make sounds. We alter the position of our mouth and tongue to shape our voice sounds into words.

The voice box or Adam's apple

Without ears we would be able to hear neither speech nor the other sounds around us. The really important parts of the ear are inside your head. The part of the ear you see is called the outer ear. The outer ear picks up sound waves caused by vibrations in the air. It leads them to the ear canal. The ear canal directs the sound waves to the eardrum.

The eardrum is a very thin skin. Sound waves make the eardrum vibrate. The ear drum passes on these vibrations to three tiny bones. These tiny bones carry the vibrations to a coiled tube which looks like a snail shell. Inside this tube are many small nerves. These carry the sound messages to the brain. The brain tells us what we have heard.

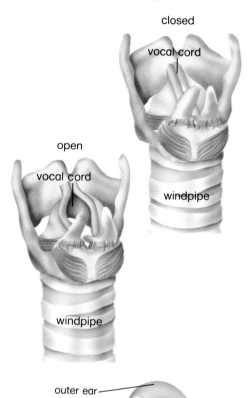

closed

vocal cord

open

vocal cord

windpipe

windpipe

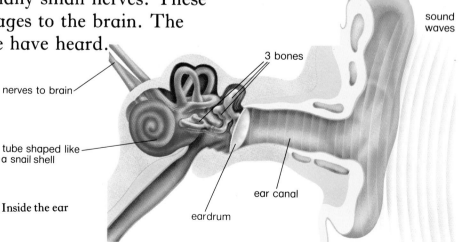

outer ear

sound waves

nerves to brain

3 bones

tube shaped like a snail shell

ear canal

Inside the ear

eardrum

Eyes and seeing

We see with our eyes. There must always be some light for us to see. We cannot see in the dark. In the center of each eye is a hole called the pupil. It is the dark part of the eye. Our pupils open up and let more light in when we are in a dim place. The pupils close up when we are in a bright place.

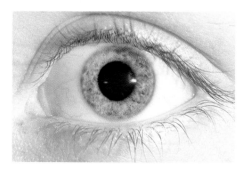

An eye in dim light

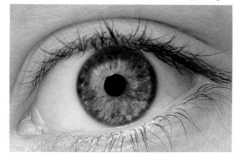

An eye in bright light

The colored part of the eye is called the iris. Behind the iris and pupil of each eye is the lens. The lens is soft like jelly. When we are looking at something, rays of light from it pass through the lens and are focused on the back of the eye. An image of what we are looking at is formed there. The back of the eye is full of nerve cells. These pass messages back to the brain telling us what we can see. The image on the back of the eye is upside down. But our brain turns the image the right way up.

muscle

pupil

iris

nerve to brain

lens

In some people, the lens of the eye is too strong or too weak to form a clear image. It is then necessary to wear spectacles to correct this. With our eyes we can see many colors. We are lucky because most animals do not see the colors we see. To a dog, cat, rabbit or horse, everything is black, white or gray.

Senses and sense organs

We can tell what is happening all around us. This is because we have sense organs that tell us what is going on. Our main sense organs are our eyes and ears. As we have seen, the eyes detect light and color and the ears are sensitive to sounds. The ears also control our sense of balance.

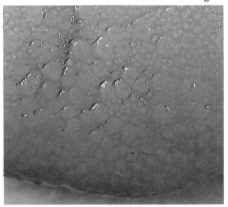

Taste buds on the tongue

But we have other sense organs as well. On our tongue there are tiny bumps called taste buds. These taste the things we eat and drink. Different parts of the tongue are sensitive to sweet, sour, bitter, and salty tastes. Your nose is sensitive to smells. Chemical substances in the air act on nerve cells inside the nose, and these send messages to the brain. A lot of what we think we taste we are really smelling. That is why food tastes so different when we have a cold.

Our sense of smell

air currents

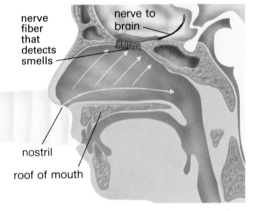

nerve fiber that detects smells

nerve to brain

nostril

roof of mouth

One of our most important sense organs is the skin. The skin has many sensitive nerve cells in it. Some of these cells are sensitive to touch. We can tell if someone touches us even if we are looking the other way. Other cells in the skin are sensitive to heat and cold. And some are sensitive to pain. Every moment of every day, messages are going from the nerve cells in our skin to our brain. These messages tell the brain what is happening to us.

Senses in the skin

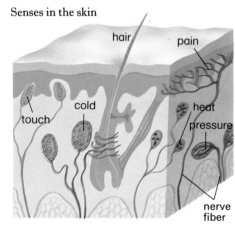

hair

pain

touch

cold

heat

pressure

nerve fiber

Nerves and the brain

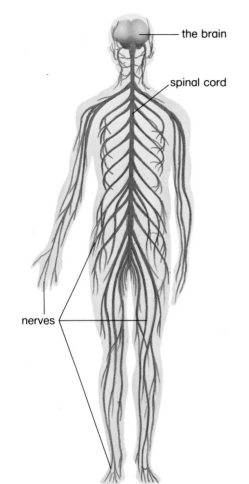

The nervous system

Labels: the brain, spinal cord, nerves

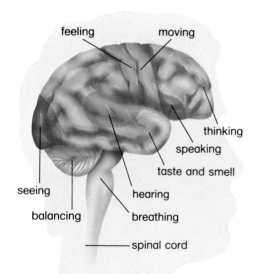

The brain, colored to show the activities it controls

Labels: feeling, moving, thinking, speaking, taste and smell, hearing, breathing, seeing, balancing, spinal cord

Everything you do, every movement you make is controlled by the brain. So is everything you think about. Your brain makes it possible for you to dream and plan, learn and remember. You walk and talk, write and read, see and hear, and laugh and cry because of your brain. Your brain controls your breathing and the beating of your heart. The brain might be called the body's control room. It sees that all the different parts of the body work together. It is better than the best computer ever made. Different parts of the brain control different parts of the body. You can see some of these in the picture.

Running down from the base of the brain through the middle of your backbone is the spinal cord. This is made of thousands of nerves. From the spinal cord nerves branch off to form a network all over the body. Messages pass down the spinal cord from the brain to all parts of the body. The brain sorts out the information in these messages. It replies with messages of its own telling the different parts of the body what action to take.

Many of the nervous messages take place without us knowing about them. For example our mouth waters when we think about something to eat. The pupils of our eyes widen when the light grows dim. If we touch a hot saucepan, we quickly pull our hand away without having to think about it.

Having babies

If people did not have children, the human race would soon become extinct. Every boy and man has two ball-shaped glands called testes lying in a bag below his penis. From the age of about 13 or 14 years these begin to produce millions of tiny cells called sperm. Inside her body a girl or woman has two ovaries, each about the size of a walnut. Between the ages of 11 and 14 years, a girl's ovaries start to produce tiny eggs. One egg is released about every 28 days.

The way in which humans produce babies is wonderful. A man and a woman who love each other very much often want to hold each other closely. The man's penis fills with blood so that it becomes hard and stiff. He is then able to insert it in the opening between the woman's legs called the vagina. Sperm is released from the penis in a liquid. The sperm swim up the woman's uterus. If there is an egg there, one of the sperm may join with the egg to form a special new cell. The egg is said to have been fertilized. We shall see on the next page how this fertilized egg grows into a baby.

Each month a woman or teenage girl's body produces an egg. The uterus gets ready to receive that egg in case it is fertilized by a sperm and grows into a baby. If that doesn't happen, then every month the egg and the lining of the uterus pass out of the vagina. This monthly flow of blood and old cells is called a period or menstruation. It is quite normal and shows a girl is growing up.

A sperm fertilizing an egg-cell

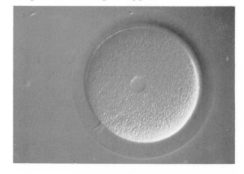

A new baby

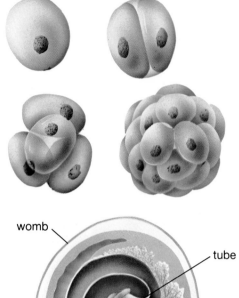

You are made of millions of cells. But you began as the special cell formed when a sperm from your father fertilized an egg from your mother. From this special cell, grew all the different cells that make up your body. This cell divides into two cells. And the two cells divide into four. The four cells divide again, and again, and again. After only two months the growing baby has its own perfect little body. It has ears, eyes, a nose, and a mouth. It has tiny arms and legs, too, and a heart that sends blood through its body.

womb

tube

water-filled bag

2in.
scale

A developing baby at ten weeks

Two months later the developing baby can suck its thumb or scratch with its own little fingernails. It even has hair on its head. The baby lives a quiet, peaceful life floating in a water-filled bag. The bag of water protects the baby from bumps and jolts and stops it from getting too hot or cold. For nine months, the growing baby gets all it needs from its mother. Food and oxygen pass from the mother's blood to the baby's blood through a special tube. Waste from the baby returns to the mother's blood for her to get rid of.

How a baby is born. Only part of one of the mother's legs is shown

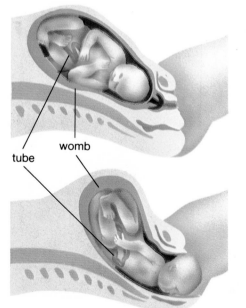

tube

womb

Just before the baby is born, the water-filled bag surrounding the baby bursts. The mother's muscles begin to push the baby out. The tube that joined the baby to its mother is cut and tied in a knot by the doctor or nurse. And a new baby is born. The navel, or belly button, shows where the baby was joined to the mother's body by the tube.

Growing up

A baby grows very quickly after it is born. At first it sleeps most of the time. It cries when it is hungry, dirty, cold, or frightened. The baby is usually fed on milk from its mother's breasts. Some babies are fed on milk from a bottle. Soon the baby learns to crawl and then to walk. It also learns to talk. By the time it is 2 years old, the baby has grown so much that it can hardly be called a baby at all.

Human children can learn much more than the young of animals. We learn to read, write, do arithmetic, play musical instruments, and hundreds of other things. Each year, as our bodies grow, we learn more and more.

Growing taller is only one way in which we grow. Our body changes in other ways. When a boy is about 13 years old his voice begins to grow deeper. Hair begins to grow on his face in the

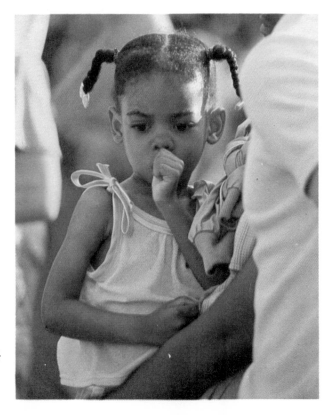

beginnings of a beard. At the age of 11 or 12 a girl's body begins to look like that of a woman. And inside the bodies of both boys and girls, important changes are taking place. These are the changes that make it possible for a girl to become a mother and for a boy to become a father.

We do not grow any taller after we are about 18 years old. But all through life we go on growing wiser and wiser as we learn more and more about the world around us.

Do you remember?

(Look for the answers in the part of the book you have just been reading if you do not know them.)

1 What is the inside of each kidney like?

2 What is the name of the watery waste liquid that comes from the kidneys?

3 What is another name for the voice box?

4 What happens when the vocal cords vibrate?

5 What is the job of the outer ear?

6 What is the eardrum made of?

7 What is the dark part of the eye called and why does its size change?

8 What is the lens of the eye like?

9 What is formed on the back of the eye when we look at something?

10 What are the tiny bumps on the tongue for?

11 What are the nerve cells in the skin sensitive to?

12 What is the spinal cord made of?

13 What would happen to the human race if people did not have children?

14 What are the ball-shaped glands called that make sperm?

15 How often does a girl or woman produce an egg?

16 What do we say has happened when a sperm joins itself to an egg?

17 What do we call it when the old lining of the uterus passes out of the vagina?

18 How is a growing baby protected inside its mother's body?

19 What happens to the tube that joined a baby to its mother when the baby is born?

20 What do very young babies feed on?

Things to do

1 **Pupils.** Work with a friend. Look into your friend's eyes when he is staring at a window or light bulb. Make a note of how big your friend's pupils are. Now ask your friend to close his eyes and cover them with his hands while he counts slowly up to 100. When he opens his eyes, look at his pupils. What difference do you notice in the pupils and the irises of his eyes?

2 **Test your eyesight.** Find a page of a newspaper or magazine that has large and small writing on it. Pin the page on a

bulletin board in your classroom. Make a mark on the floor 9ft. 7in. from the newspaper or magazine page. Try to read the page. Use first your right eye, then your left eye, then both eyes. How much can you read? Do your friends do better or worse than you do? If any of your friends wear glasses, ask them to do the test, first of all without the glasses and then with them. What differences are there?

3   Our sense of smell. Put two or three drops of perfume on a clean handkerchief. Take a deep sniff of the perfume. Go on sniffing it for a few minutes. What happens to the smell? Why is this?

4   Sense of touch. Take a sharpened pencil. Gently touch the point of it against the skin on your palms and the backs of your hands, the soles of your feet, your neck and forehead, your elbow and arm. Are some places more sensitive to touch than others? Which places are the most sensitive? Which are the least sensitive?

5   Clinical thermometers. Ask your teacher or some other grown-up to show you a clinical thermometer. This is the kind of thermometer used by doctors and nurses to find the temperature of the body.

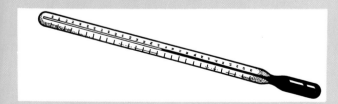

How does this kind of thermometer work? Why does the doctor or nurse usually shake the thermometer? What is the usual temperature of the body? What happens to the temperature of the body when you are ill?

6   You as a baby. Try to find out how much you weighed when you were born. How much do you weigh now? How many times heavier are you now than when you were born?

Find out how long you were when you were born. How tall are you now? How many times longer (or taller) are you now than when you were born?

7   Measuring heights and weights. How tall are the children in your class? Start by measuring everyone. Who is the tallest? Who is the shortest? Put your results on a graph like this:

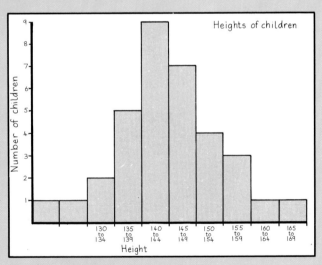

Which height group has the most children in it?

Work out the average height of the boys and the average height of the girls in your class. Is there a difference? Which group is bigger?

Weigh everyone in your class or group. Who is the lightest? Who is the heaviest? Make a graph of your results like this:

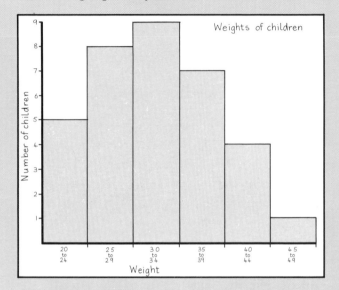

Which weight group has the most children in it? Does the average weight of the boys differ from the average weight of the girls?

If possible compare your graphs for height and weight with those made by another class with children of different ages.

Experiments to try

Do your experiments carefully. Write or draw what you have done and what happens. Say what you have learned. Compare your findings with those of your friends.

1 Why are long bones hollow?

As we saw on page 4, long bones are hollow. You can see why if you do this simple experiment.

What you need: A sheet of thick paper; two books, both the same size; coins or beads; tape; a tin lid.

What you do: A sheet of paper is light but it is not strong. Put a sheet of paper between the two books like this. How many beads or coins can you put on the paper before it collapses?

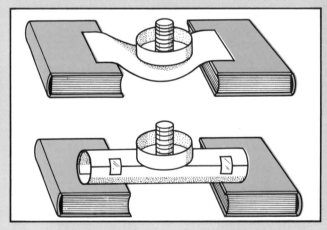

Now roll up the sheet of paper. This shape, like a pipe or a long bone, is called a hollow cylinder. Fix the ends with tape. How many coins or beads can you put on the paper now before it collapses?

Where else, other than in the body, have you seen hollow cylinders being used because they are strong but light?

2 How hard can you push with one foot?

What you need: A bathroom scale. Ask a friend to help you.

What you do: Stand the bathroom scale against a wall like this.

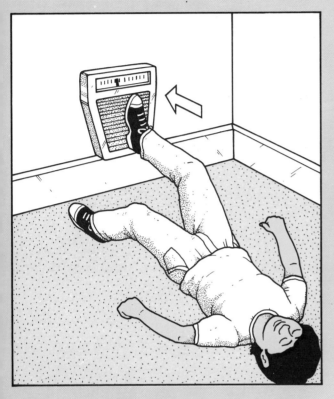

Put one foot flat against the scale. Push the scale as hard as you can. Ask your friend to read the scale while you are pushing it. Try to feel which muscles are helping you push. Record how hard you pushed.

Do the experiment again. This time use the other foot. With which foot did you push the hardest?

Now let your friend have a turn. Which of you pushed harder with the left foot? Which of you pushed harder with the right foot?

Now see who can grip harder with both hands. Grip the bathroom scale to find out.

3   How strong is a hair?

What you need: Tape; a strip of paper about 1 inch wide; small nails or paper clips; a long hair.

What you do: Stick one end of a long hair to a shelf or door frame with tape. Stick the other end of the hair to the ends of the strip of paper. The picture shows you how to do this.

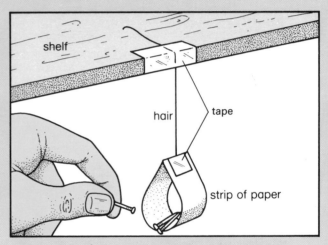

shelf

hair

tape

strip of paper

Put small nails or paper clips (all the same size) – one at a time – into the paper.

How many nails or paper clips do you add before the hair breaks?

Now do the experiment with a hair from someone else. Who has the strongest hair?

4   How fast do you breathe?

What you need: A watch or clock with a second hand; a friend to help you.

What you do: Sit down quietly on a chair and ask your friend to see how many times you breathe each minute. It is best to do this three times and to find the average of the three counts.

Find out how many breaths you take in a minute after you have:

(a) been standing for 5 minutes
(b) walked quickly around the playground
(c) run around the playground
(d) jumped up and down for a few minutes.

Show your results on a block graph or histogram.

What do you notice about the number of times you breathe each minute after you have carried out these various exercises? When do you breathe the fastest? When do you breathe the slowest?

Now change places with your friend. Does your friend breathe faster or slower than you did after doing the exercises? Is your friend bigger or smaller than you are? Is your friend better or not as good at games than you are?

5   How much air do your lungs hold?

Do this experiment with your teacher.

What you need: A large plastic bottle that holds 1 gallon; a large bowl; a piece of rubber tubing about 24 inches long; a glass containing a weak antiseptic solution; a ruler; some rubber bands.

What you do: Fill the bottle to the top with water. Put some water in the bowl (not too much, or it will overflow later). Hold your hand tightly over the top of the bottle of water. Quickly but carefully turn the bottle upside down so that the top is under the water in the bowl. Take your

hand off the top of the bottle. Ask someone to hold the bottle steady for you. Fix a ruler to the side of the bottle with rubber bands.

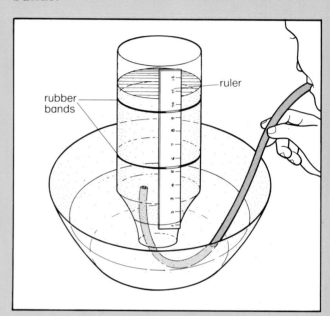

Put the tube in the neck of the bottle, as shown in the picture. Take a deep breath. Hold your nose, and blow down the tube. The more air you have in your lungs, the more water you can blow out of the bottle. Measure the distance between the bottom (now the top!) of the bottle and the level of the water.

How much air do your lungs hold? When do you breathe deeply like this?

Instead of taking the biggest breath you can, just take an ordinary one. How much smaller is this ordinary breath than the bigger one?

Who has the biggest lungs in your class? After each person has blown down the tube, dip the end in a weak solution of antiseptic to kill any germs. Do the biggest people have the largest lungs? Do the smallest people have the smallest lungs? Are the people with the largest lungs better at running, swimming, or games than those with the smaller lungs?

6 Why do we have two eyes?

What you need: Two pencils.

What you do: Close one eye. Point one finger at something in the distance. Look along your finger with the eye you still have open.

Now close that eye and open the other. Hold your finger still. Is your finger still pointing at the same place?

Hold one pencil in each hand. Hold them so that the points are enclosed in your hands. Close one eye. Can you make the two ends of the pencils touch while holding them at arms' length? Now try with both eyes open. Is it easier to make the pencils touch with one eye open or with both?

Write down why you think you need two eyes.

7 How does exercise affect your pulse?

What you need: A watch or clock with a second hand.

What you do: Sit still for three minutes so that your pulse settles down to a steady beat. Then use a watch or clock that shows seconds to count how many times your heart beats in a minute.

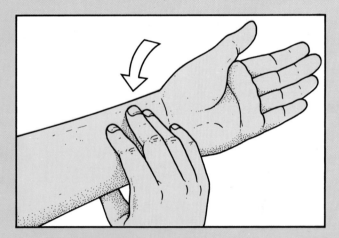

You can take your pulse if you place the middle finger of your right hand lightly on your left wrist. Put your middle finger in the place shown in the picture. Or you can take your pulse with the pulse counter on page 16. Take your pulse while you are sitting twice more, and find the average.

Now either run around the playground or run in place for three or four minutes. Again take your pulse.

Rest for a few minutes and then do the exercise and take your pulse twice more. Work out the average pulse.

What effect does exercise have on your pulse? What reasons for this can you think of?

Glossary

Here are the meanings of some words you might have met for the first time in this book.

Anus: the opening from the digestive system where waste food leaves the body.

Arteries: tubes that carry blood away from the heart.

Bladder: bag-like organ that stores urine from the kidneys.

Blood circulation: the way in which blood travels around the body, as it is pumped by the heart.

Canines: the pointed teeth that tear and shred food.

Capillaries: very small blood vessels that connect the smallest arteries and veins.

Cells: the tiny building blocks that make up plants and animals. Humans and all living things are made up of cells.

Diaphragm: a large sheet of muscle that separates the chest from the lower part of the body.

Digestion: the breaking up of food into tiny pieces that can pass into the blood.

Fertilization: the joining up of a sperm (the male cells) with an egg (a female cell).

Incisors: the front teeth that are used for biting and cutting food.

Intestines: the lower part of the long tube in which food is digested and from where it passes into the blood.

Iris: the colored part of the eye.

Joints: the joining of separate bones in the skeleton to allow movement.

Lung: a thin-walled bag containing many tubes and air sacs, where oxygen from the air passes into the blood.

Marrow: the jellylike substance inside bone where red blood cells are made.

Melanin: the dark coloring matter in some cells in the skin.

Menstruation: in women, the monthly passing from the body of the old lining of the uterus and an egg that has not been fertilized.

Molars and premolars: the back teeth that are used for crushing and grinding food.

Ovaries: the glands in which females produce eggs.

Penis: the fleshy tube between a boy or man's legs that is used to pass urine and to place sperm in a female's body.

Period: see menstruation.

Pupil: the small black opening in the center of the iris of the eye.

Skeleton: the internal framework of bones, or the external shell that supports or protects an animal's body.

Sperm: tiny male cells that are necessary to fertilize an egg and produce a baby.

Spinal cord: the bundle of nerves that runs through the backbone from the brain.

Sweat: moisture that comes from pores in the skin.

Taste buds: the little red bumps on the tongue with which we taste our food.

Tendon: white string-like strands that join muscles to bones.

Testes: (Singular: **testis**) male sperm-producing glands.

Urine: the waste water containing unwanted chemicals that is passed out from the bladder.

Uterus: the thick tube of muscle in a woman's body in which a fertilized egg grows into a baby.

Vagina: the passage between a girl or woman's legs that leads to the uterus.

Veins: tubes in which blood travels back to the heart.

Vibration: the rapid movement to and fro of something that may produce sounds.

Vocal cords: tiny bands of muscle inside the voice box that vibrate when we speak.

Voice box: the lump in our throat, the Adam's apple, with which we speak.

Womb: the thick tube of muscle in a woman's body in which a fertilized egg-cell grows into a baby.

Acknowledgments

The publishers would like to thank the following for permission to reproduce transparencies:

All Sport/David Cannon: pII (top right); Mary Evans Picture Library: p.20 (top); Biophoto Associates: p17 (top); Terry Jennings: p9 (bottom), p18 (top); Mothercare: p24 (2nd from top); Oxford Scientific Films: p20 (2nd from top); Chris Ridgers: back cover (top), p5 (right), p6 (center); Science Photo Library/Martin Dohrn: p19 (top and 2nd from top); Science Photo Library/Eric Grave: back cover (bottom), p12 (top); Science Photo Library/Dr G. Schatten: p22 (bottom); Scotland Yard: p14 (right); Spectrum Colour Library; front cover (center left), p6 (top), p24 (top); Sporting Pictures: p5 (left and middle); Tony Stone Associates: front cover (top right and bottom left), p1, p3 (top and bottom), p25 (top).

Illustrations by Mike Saunders, Wendy Brett, Karen Daws, David Eaton, Edward McLachlan and Barrie Thorpe.

Index